Germany

Helen Arnold

RAINTREE STECK-VAUGHN
PUBLISHERS
The Steck-Vaughn Company

Austin, Texas

Published by Raintree Steck-Vaughn Publishers, an imprint of Steck-Vaughn Company

A ZOË BOOK

Editor: Kath Davies, Helene Resky
Design: Jan Sterling, Sterling Associates
Map: Gecko Limited
Production: Grahame Griffiths

Library of Congress Cataloging-in-Publication Data

Arnold, Helen.
    Germany / Helen Arnold.
        p. cm. — (Postcards from)
    Includes index.
    ISBN 0-8172-4008-X (lib. binding)
    ISBN 0-8172-4229-5 (softcover)
    1. Germany — Description and travel — Juvenile literature.
    2. Postcards — Germany — Juvenile Literature. [1. Germany — Description and travel.] I. Title. II. Series.
    DD43.A83 1996
    943–dc20
                            95–16215
                                CIP
                                AC

Printed and bound in the United States
  3 4 5 6 7 8 9 0 WZ 99

Photographic acknowledgments

The publishers wish to acknowledge, with thanks, the following photographic sources:

The Hutchison Library / Vladimir Birgus 8; / J.G. Fuller 10; Robert Harding Picture Library / Nigel Blythe - title page; / Adina Tovy 26; Impact Photos / Piers Cavendish 22; / Fabrizio Bensch 28; Zefa - cover, 6, 12, 14, 16, 18, 20, 24.

The publishers have made every effort to trace the copyright holders, but if they have inadvertently overlooked any, they will be pleased to make the necessary arrangement at the first opportunity.

Contents

All the words that appear in **bold** are explained in the Glossary on page 30.

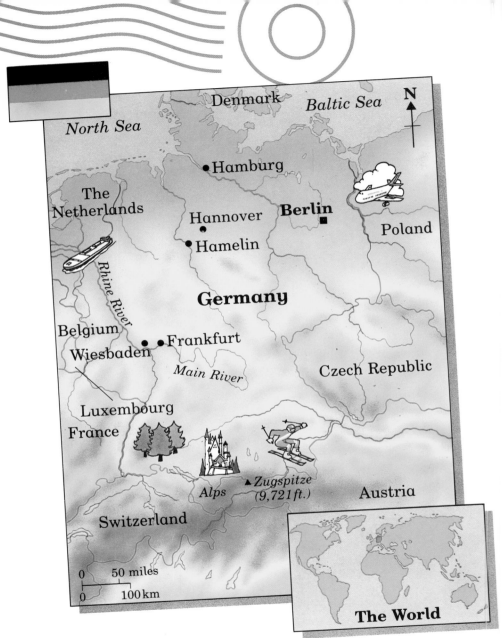

North Sea
Denmark
Baltic Sea
N

The
Netherlands

● Hamburg

Hannover
●

Berlin

Poland

● Hamelin

Rhine River

Germany

Belgium
Wiesbaden

● ● Frankfurt

Main River

Czech Republic

Luxembourg
France

Alps
▲ *Zugspitze (9,721 ft.)*

Austria

Switzerland

0 50 miles
0 100 km

The World

A big map of Germany
and a small map of the world

Dear Emma,

You can see Germany in red on the small map. It is in northern Europe. Germany is very far from Dallas, Texas. Our plane took about nine hours to get here.

Love,

Ann

P.S. Dad has been looking at the map. He says that Berlin is a lot farther north than Dallas. The weather here is much cooler than at home.

The Brandenburg Gate, Berlin

Dear Thomas,

This famous building goes across a big road in the middle of Berlin. It is more than 200 years old. It is called the Brandenburg Gate. It doesn't look like a gate!

Yours,

Alex

P.S. Mom says that after Germany lost the last war, it was split into two parts. Now it is one country again, and Berlin is the **capital** city.

The Ku'damm, Berlin

Dear Linda,

This street in Berlin has a very long name. It is called the Ku'damm for short. Lots of people meet here to go shopping. I have some German money called *marks*.

Love,

Jenny

P.S. Many German people speak very good English. Mom says I should learn German. Some German words look very long. Some of the writing looks different from English.

Sausages and cold meats for sale in Wiesbaden

Dear Carl,

Some stores in Germany sell hundreds of different **sausages**. I like *frankfurters*. Mom buys cream puffs from the bakery. People here often buy cakes as presents.

Your friend,

Dan

P.S. Our German friends come from a town called Hamburg. That is where hamburgers come from. Can you guess where *frankfurters* come from?

Gutenfels Castle on the Rhine River

Dear Lee,

The Rhine River is more than 800 miles (1,290 km) long. It flows from the Swiss mountains right through Germany toward the ocean. It reaches the North Sea in the Netherlands.

Your friend,

Martina

P.S. Uncle Jon says that people live on the **barges** that take **goods** along the Rhine. It takes 8 days for a barge to get from Switzerland to the Netherlands.

The town square in Hamelin

Dear Suzannah,

Do you know the story of the Pied Piper? This is the town where he got rid of all the rats. He walked out of the town playing his pipe. The rats went with him because they liked the music.

Love,

Mary

P.S. Mom says that lots of stories come from Germany. Some of these **legends** are very old. I like *Little Red Riding Hood* best.

Neuschwanstein Castle in the
Bavarian Alps

Dear Rick,

We are in the Alps. These mountains are very high. This part of southern Germany is called Bavaria. There are many lakes and castles. We went to see the castle in the picture.

See you soon,

Mike

P.S. Grandpa says that this castle is 100 years old. It was built by King Ludwig of Bavaria. Some people said he was crazy!

Frankfurt, on the Main River

Dear Sasha,

Most people here live and work in new, high buildings. It is a very clean city. The roads are full of traffic. We like to travel on the **subway**. It is called the *U-bahn*.

Love,

Mandy

P.S. Dad says that many people in Frankfurt work for banks. There must be a lot of money here!

A wild boar in the Black Forest

Dear Joe,

We went on a trip to the Black Forest. We saw millions of tall trees. We looked for a wild **boar**, but we did not find one. Mom drove very fast on the German **highways**. They are called *autobahnen*.

Your friend,

Keith

P.S. Dad says that people can drive very fast on the *autobahn*. Maybe that is why the Germans make very fast cars!

A German high-speed train at
Hannover station

Dear Shirley,

This train can go much faster than a car. It is one of the new high-speed trains. The German people are very good at making trains and cars. They make all kinds of machines.

Love,

Richard

P.S. Mom says that German children work hard at school. They have lots of homework. When they leave school, they can go to a **university** or get a job.

Skiing in the Zugspitze Alps

Dear Nina,

We are skiing near the highest mountain in Germany. It is very cold, and there is a lot of snow. Many German people come here every weekend in the winter. They are good at skiing.

Your friend,

Carlos

P.S. Dad says that German families like to take summer vacations by the ocean. They go to hot places, such as Spain and Greece.

The children's festival

Dear Sue,

Yesterday was a special day for children. They dressed up for a **festival**. There was music and dancing in the streets. We all went to watch.

Love,

Kirsty

P.S. My friend Johann says that most people in Germany are **Christians**. They have festivals at Easter and Christmas. The Germans were the first people to have Christmas trees.

The German flag flying over
the Reichstag

Dear Barry,

About 200 years ago German soldiers won a battle against Napoleon, the **emperor** of France. The soldiers wore **uniforms** of red, black, and gold. These colors are on the German flag today.

Your friend,

Nathan

P.S. Dad says that kings once ruled parts of Germany. Now the people choose their own leaders. The leaders meet at the Reichstag. Germany is a **democracy**.

Glossary

Barge: A long boat that has a flat bottom. Barges are used to carry heavy goods.

Boar: A wild pig

Capital: The town or city where people who rule the country meet. The capital is not always the biggest city in the country.

Christians: People who follow the teachings of Jesus. Jesus lived about 2,000 years ago.

Democracy: A country where the people choose the leaders they want to run the country

Emperor: A man who rules several different countries

Festival: A time when people celebrate something or someone special from the past. People often dance and sing during a festival.

Goods: Things that can be sold

Highway: A large main road that helps people get from one place to another more directly

Legend: An old story that many people believe, even though it may not be true

P.S.: This stands for Post Script which means "to write after." A postscript is the part of a card or letter that is added at the end, after the person has signed it.

Sausage: A skin tube filled with meat

Subway: A train that runs under the ground

Uniform: The special clothes that a group of people wear so that they all look the same

University: A place where people go to study after high school

Index